TORONTO
DISCOVERED

TORONTO DISCOVERED

Robert Fulford

KEY PORTER BOOKS

Canadian Cataloguing in Publication Data

Fulford, Robert, 1932–
    Toronto discovered

ISBN 1-55013-939-8

1. Toronto (Ont.). 2. Toronto (Ont.) — Pictorial works. I. Title

FC3097.3.F84 1998   971.3'541   C98-930260-1
F1059.5.T68F8 1998

THE CANADA COUNCIL | LE CONSEIL DES ARTS
FOR THE ARTS | DU CANADA
SINCE 1957 | DEPUIS 1957

The publisher gratefully acknowledges the support of the Canada Council for the Arts and the Ontario Arts Council for its publishing program.

Key Porter Books Limited
70 The Esplanade
Toronto, Ontario
Canada M5E 1R2

DESIGN: Jack Steiner
PHOTOGRAPHS: **Daniel Dutka**: pages 12, 19, 24, 25, 28 (upper and lower), 30, 31, 34, 37, 40, 42, 47, 53, 55, 57, 58, 62, 63 (upper), 64 (upper), 65, 75 (upper and lower), 78, 82 (lower), 83, 87 (lower), 98, 102 (upper and lower), 103, 104, 105; **Malak Photographs Ltd.**: pages 8, 16, 20, 23, 26–27, 60, 84, 106 (upper), 107; **Ontario Tourism**: pages 59 (upper and lower), 61 (lower), 86; **Tim Peters**, © 1998: pages 18, 54, 85; **Zeidler Roberts Partnership Architects (photographer: Balthazar Korab)**: page 36; **Chris Snell Photography**: pages 9, 32, 33, 35 (upper and lower), 38, 39, 41, 43, 44, 45, 46 (upper and lower), 48 (upper and lower), 49, 50, 51, 63 (lower), 67, 68 (upper and lower), 69, 71, 73 (lower, left and right), 74, 76, 77 (upper and lower), 81 (lower), 83 (upper), 88, 95, 96, 97, 99, 100 (upper), 101; **Tourism Toronto**: pages 6, 11, 13, 14, 15, 17, 21, 29, 52, 56, 61 (upper), 64 (lower), 66, 70, 72, 73 (upper), 79, 80, 81 (upper), 87 (upper), 90 (upper and lower), 91 (upper and lower), 92, 93, 94, 100 (lower), 106 (lower).

Printed and bound in Canada

98 99 00 01 02 6 5 4 3 2 1

CONTENTS

INTRODUCTION

AN UNDISCOVERED REGION, a tantalizing puzzle of a city, Toronto unfolds as a chain of surprises, startling locals and visitors alike. What can we say of a place that has somehow managed to establish *four* Chinatowns? How can we understand a metropolis that's built itself inside a park and wrapped around a university? In Toronto, even the topography is a bit of a secret: hundreds of dark, leafy ravines, mainly hidden from the streets, are unknown to all but the most inquisitive visitors. Once the plain Jane of North American municipalities, Toronto has developed into a dense collection of urban mysteries, where buried rivers and a maze of tunnels beneath the downtown skyscrapers (given the enigmatic title "PATH") await discovery by devoted pilgrims. And Toronto never stands still, not for a minute. When people begin talking about Toronto they always utter the word *change*, and they never fail to say how different it is, how *surprisingly* different, from the Toronto they knew thirty years ago, or ten years ago, or just the other day.

Toronto reinvents itself on the run. It's a city in motion, chronically unfinished, forever inventing new patterns of commerce and human settlement as it rushes eagerly toward its destiny (whatever that may be). If you ignore a certain district for a few years, you may well discover, upon returning, that it's been abruptly transformed. A dowdy old neighbourhood has suddenly become chic, filled with cool restaurants and young men with earrings playing pool in black shirts. Or a street that was clearly Portuguese has lately decided (who knows how such decisions are made?) to turn Vietnamese. Or a once-crumbling warehouse district has filled up (overnight, so it seems) with hundreds of frantic little companies that could not have existed until recently, all bearing names that emerge from the same DNA pool of the imagination—Softcom Technology, Digital Music Inc., Magic Online Services, XBase Technologies. etc. And if ethnic and business districts change swiftly, so does the city's sexual geography. In the mid-1990s Torontonians had just become accustomed to recognizing Church Street as the downtown gay district (and focus of the annual Gay Pride Day) when they began to realize that the community was spreading eastward, across the Don Valley, making the once-humdrum old residential streets of Riverdale into what's now sometimes called "gayburb."

Most of these changes expand the city's human repertoire and its range of expression. They make it more diverse, more open and, on its best days, more welcoming. Once, ambitious Torontonians dreamt of going to distant corners of the world. They still do, but even if they stay put the world now comes to Toronto—and Toronto, dazzled by its good fortune, does all it can to celebrate this fact. Municipal street signs in certain districts announce the origin of the people who live there (or did live there, when the signs went up, a few years ago). Signs that say "Rua Acores," for instance, designate a stretch of Dundas Street West as the place where Portuguese from the Azores settled. Signs announcing "Corso Italia" define the empire of gelatto bars on St. Clair Avenue West as a spiritual colony of Italy. On Danforth Avenue, where the brilliant designs of Greek restaurants have brought vivid life to a once-dozy boulevard, street signs use the Greek alphabet. It doesn't matter that a majority of the Greeks who arrived there two or three decades ago have since moved on. They were kind enough to leave behind a charming piece of their identity.

Toronto often claims to be the most multicultural city on the planet; certainly it has a higher proportion of Asians than any other Western city not on the Pacific. Anne Michaels, in her prize-winning novel *Fugitive Pieces*, calls Toronto "a city where almost everyone has come from elsewhere—a market, a caravansary—bringing with them their different ways of dying and marrying, their kitchens and songs." Once, Torontonians preferred to ignore or blur the differences between ethnic groups, assuming that in any case they would one day all be the same. But since the 1970s the city's instinct has been the opposite: it wants to announce the multitude of ethnic groups in the city, define them, and invite them to the party. And in this case, "party" is often meant literally: Toronto has become dedicated to celebrating itself. In summer and autumn, Toronto's good seasons (winter can be harsh, spring pathetically brief), the city makes a point of enjoying itself in public, and invites visitors to do the same. It's a place that loves festivals—the jazz festival, the underground theatre festival, the poetry-readings festival, the Caribana parade, and

Once each summer, Toronto's black community asserts its identity in the explosive splendour of the Caribana parade.

(above all) the film festival, which every autumn turns downtown Toronto into a *Cinema Paradiso* for ten days of ecstasy in the dark.

Toronto was not always this way, to put it mildly. As recently as mid-century, many found the old British-bred Toronto a nice place to live and work, but few suggested you might want to go there for pleasure. It was not famously sociable, no one bragged about the restaurants, the city's cultural interests were muted, and there were those who freely applied to Toronto the adjective "cold"—all year round. For a good time, people stayed home: pleasure was a private matter. Everyone admitted that Montreal was friendlier, more cosmopolitan, and an incomparably better place to eat.

In those days, change moved across the surface of Toronto as slowly as the great shield of ice that covered this part of the world until, twelve millennia ago, it finally slid away. For many a long bleak year, Toronto was dominated by grim-faced Puritans who made the Christian Sabbath a day of such stifling silent piety that it became infamous across the British Commonwealth. This was a new Ice Age, as those who lived through it can still attest. The Lord's Day Alliance, a ferociously effective lobby formed in 1888 under Presbyterian leadership, zealously enforced the Lord's Day Act, which made everything from Sunday movies to Sunday professional baseball—and above all, public consumption of alcoholic beverages—absolutely unlawful. On Sunday, some people went to church to express their faith. Others went out of desperation, for entertainment.

Ancient Torontonians, those who have lived here all their lives, can remember the great political debate of the 1950s about the morality, or immorality, of holding sports events on Sundays. In those days, self-denial was first among Toronto virtues—and not just on Sunday. To buy a bottle of whisky you went to a government store and signed your name to a piece of paper. Sidewalk cafés were not only illegal, they were unthinkable. Who in the world, people asked, would *want* to sit outside, eating and drinking under the gaze of strangers, when a perfectly proper and discreetly dark restaurant was available inside?

On Saturday mornings, the St. Lawrence Market on Front Street becomes the favourite meeting place for downtown Torontonians.

It was the worldwide prosperity of the 1950s and 1960s that finally broke the Puritan grip and made a more relaxed urban life possible. Toronto came to understand that it could no longer keep up if it lived by rules that most of Europe and America thought laughable. The city began changing in the 1950s, around the same time it moved clearly ahead of Montreal as the commercial capital of Canada. The rules fell, one by one. Large-scale immigration, first of all from Italy, helped. When the Hungarian revolution of 1956 failed, Toronto was a beneficiary: ever since, Hungarians who came in the 1950s have been a potent force in Toronto life. Greek and Portuguese immigrants followed. In 1964, when the English writer V. S. Pritchett visited Toronto to prepare a travel piece for an American magazine, he noted that Toronto was still notorious for obsessive propriety; but, he said, "the first thing a Toronto man tells you today is that all this has changed." That was true, but far bigger changes were just ahead. The liberalized immigration rules introduced by the federal government in the mid-1960s opened Canada to immigrants from regions previously restricted, including the Caribbean, Africa, and South Asia. That affected many parts of Canada, but Toronto most of all. By the 1970s, Toronto was on the way to becoming what it is today—a meeting place for all the races of the planet and in many ways as great a surprise to native-born Torontonians as it is to any visitor.

A WALK THAT STARTS at Dundas Street and University Avenue provides one way to see Toronto in motion and at the same time glimpse the pre-modern city. Dundas and University is the northeast corner of the new downtown Toronto, which reaches west to Spadina Avenue and south to the waterfront. Change has come swiftly to many sections of the city, but this is where change has been most spectacular, partly because much of this land lay commercially fallow for the first seven decades of the 20th century and has only recently come to life. It now contains the CN Tower, the SkyDome, the CBC Broadcasting Centre, Roy Thomson Hall, the Princess of Wales Theatre, several hundred restaurants, and a good deal more. This complexity can't be quickly grasped, but you can absorb the mixture of public styles, and acquire some feeling for the essential Toronto, in a walk of about eighteen blocks—along Dundas to Spadina Avenue, then south on Spadina to Queen Street, then back east as far as Bay Street.

The walking itself takes only about forty-five minutes, but the journey should properly consume most of an easygoing day, with plenty of pit stops for food, art, shopping, drink, and other necessities. These eighteen blocks demonstrate what Toronto was, what it has become, and perhaps a little of what it will be.

Towering over University Avenue, Walter Allward's 1910 monument memorializes Canadians who died for the Empire in the Boer War.

On the south side of Dundas, Chinese ideograms appear on a large glass window of the 52 Division station of the Metropolitan Police, built in 1977 to an early post-modern design that echoes early-20th-century Deco style. Those ideograms, and a few Chinese stores in the next block, are hints of much more to come. But first, *Two Forms*, the gigantic Henry Moore sculpture sitting on the sidewalk at McCaul Street, announces the city's most remarkable collection of modern art, the Henry Moore Sculpture Centre, inside the Art Gallery of Ontario. This is the largest Moore collection on public exhibit anywhere, in a space designed by Moore himself. The Art Gallery, which has been building

On Dundas Street West, Henry Moore's massive **Two Forms** *advertises the presence of the Henry Moore Sculpture Centre inside the AGO.*

and rebuilding itself on this site for most of the 20th century (the current version dates from 1992), will reward a few hours of attention. The Canadian collection is vast and exhaustive, the modern European and American light but impressive, the Old Masters relatively few in number but interesting.

A visitor who enters the Art Gallery and heads to the back of the building can visit the Grange and walk right into Toronto (and Canadian) history. The Grange is an elegant Georgian mansion, built around 1818 by one of the city's leading families, on what was then a 100-acre estate (there's still a modest park at the back). The exquisite restoration, executed in the 1970s, captures the Grange at a moment of glory, when the Family Compact socialized here in the 1820s and 1830s, exercising over the tiny British colony around them a dictatorship of taste and political power. Their arrogance inspired the rage that led to William Lyon Mackenzie's rebellion of 1837, which in turn produced the first stirring of democracy in this corner of the world. In the late 19th century, the Grange became the mansion of Goldwin Smith, a former Oxford professor of English whose prolific and controversial writing made him a renowned political journalist. Smith and his wife left the Grange to the public as the basis of an art museum.

The flickering neon sculpture on the west side of the Art Gallery at Beverley Street is *All Things Being Equal*, made by Michael Hayden in 1978, when avant-garde sculptors imagined they could use electricity for their own ends, not yet quite aware that the possibilities of coloured light were already in the hands of advertising display artists. After nightfall, this section of Dundas Street makes that point vividly clear—it becomes a place of intense urban beauty, the vivid oriental neon signs making it look (to Western eyes) just like a section of Hong Kong or Shanghai.

At Beverley Street, Dundas becomes densely Chinese, or in some cases Vietnamese. This is the old Chinatown, moved westward. Generations ago, Chinese commerce in Toronto clustered around Elizabeth Street, but in the 1960s

One of four Toronto Chinatowns makes a section of Dundas Street, near Spadina, look like an animated city in Asia.

it was displaced by the New City Hall and related buildings. There were grieving Torontonians who imagined this displacement would mean the death of Chinatown, which had been one of the liveliest sections of town for decades. Instead, Chinatown reconfigured itself, adopted Spadina Avenue as its new focus, and became much larger. The Dragon City Mall, on the west side of Spadina at Dundas, and the China Town Centre, two blocks to the south, are among many results of the recent waves of immigration from China. There's another Chinatown in the city (like this one, it has street signs in Chinese), at Gerrard Street East and Broadview Avenue; and the suburbs have created two more. The Chinatown in the eastern suburb of Scarborough, around Sheppard Avenue and

Victoria Park, has a large commercial centre and the greatest concentration of Chinese population. The fourth Chinatown, in the western suburb of Mississaugua, is smaller but still impressive, and takes the Dragon's Gate shopping centre (at Dundas and the Dixie Road) as its centre.

Walking south on Spadina Avenue, a visitor could imagine for a moment that the city had become entirely oriental: there are few other signs of commercial life. But at Queen Street, Chinatown abruptly ends, and you turn east (that is, left) into an entirely different world, moving from one culture to another in a twinkling, each of them sharply defined. Queen West has become one of Toronto's cultural legends, the centre of avant-garde art and advanced body-piercing, a place where consumerism and cultural theory live uneasily together. It emerged in the 1970s as a new Bohemia, a place of art galleries, bookstores, obscure restaurants and bars, many of them hangouts for art students (the Ontario College of Art and Design is nearby) and other pioneers of nose jewellery. As the cooking in the restaurants improved, the crowds gathered, and moneyed, middle-class Toronto decided the artists made the street colourful. Rents increased, and many of those who saw themselves as creators of the district discovered they were

Funk Central, Queen Street West, provides a focus for artists and other post-graduate students of advanced body-piercing.

being priced out of it by the famous logos. (They moved on, ever westward. In the 1990s the locals gave the name West of West to the part of Queen Street that stretches beyond Spadina. How far does it go? No one knows, since apparently it grows slowly longer every day.)

This apparently inevitable sequence of urban events, acted out a generation before on Yorkville Avenue, has left Toronto with a wonderfully engaging street; probably there is no other strip in this region which so richly repays the visitor who makes a detailed street-level exploration. From Spadina eastward, the strip unfolds, first of all as a series of bars and restaurants—places that are famous for country music in one case, avant-garde rock in another, World Beat in a third. There you will find a collection of bistros, where often the food will be Thai Toronto, which is Toronto's idea of California's idea of what people in Thailand would eat if they had the money.

At John Street the visitor encounters an intense cluster of culture. Across the street, on the southeast corner of Queen and John, 299 Queen Street West encapsulates in one building the history of Toronto taste. It went up in 1915 to house the Methodist Book and Publishing Company, later called the Ryerson Press; that explains the neo-Gothic design atop the façade and the grotesque sculptures of readers and scribes. In the 1980s it became the ChumCity Building, and it now houses an empire of electronic taste—MuchMusic, Citytv, and Bravo!, the arts channel. Near St. Patrick Street, on the north side, a much smaller sign in a restaurant sometimes demonstrates a typically Toronto multiculturalism: "Sushi Salad & Toasted Bagel."

At University Avenue there's another refined Georgian monument to 19th century Toronto, Chief Justice William Campbell's house, built in 1822 for a man who came to Canada from Scotland as a soldier and ended up as chief justice of Upper Canada. It sat first on Adelaide Street and in 1972 was moved to this location with great difficulty and much ceremony, to serve as the home of the Advocates Society.

When you cross University Avenue (to the south is Emanuel Hahn's 1933 monument to Adam Beck, who created Ontario Hydro)

On Queen Street, the elegant 1822 house of a famous judge has been turned into the headquarters of a society of lawyers.

Once, Osgoode Hall's odd little gates excluded roaming cows while admitting lawyers. They're retained for their quaintness.

you arrive at Osgoode Hall, a Palladian-Georgian building named after William Osgoode, the first chief justice of the province. Built in the early 1830s, but much altered since, Osgoode Hall remains the centre of the high courts of justice and one of the most elegant old buildings of the city. A souvenir of the early days has been left to remind us that there was farmland near here when Osgoode Hall went up: those odd-looking gates are cleverly designed to permit human entry while keeping cows from straying onto the grounds.

At Bay Street this tour ends with a beginning: the New City Hall, designed by Viljo Revell of Finland after an international competition. Nathan Phillips Square, which starts at Queen Street, has acquired an unfortunately cluttered look, apparently because no idea to insert something into it is ever rejected—it has a Peace Garden, a statue of Winston Churchill, another garden whose meaning is obscure, and a stage that is always being erected for that night's concert. But the building itself—two sculptured concrete towers of unequal size, embracing the mushroom-shaped council chamber—remains the most important structure erected in Toronto in the 20th century. In a rather stodgy city, when the new immigration laws had not yet taken effect, the Revell city hall opened up a multitude of possibilities for architecture and many other things. It said that Toronto was open to the new, was not predictable, was ready for risk. Few buildings in Canada have ever spoken so loudly, so clearly, so effectively. It was here, one magical day in 1965, that the new Toronto was born.

In the New City Hall, beyond the arches of the reflecting pool on Nathan Phillips Square, the spirit of Toronto was renewed and refreshed in the 1960s.

INTRODUCTION

Downtown: The Layered City on the Shore Plain

HERE ARE THOSE who call BCE Place the loveliest skyscraper complex in Toronto. There are those who call it the ugliest. Both arguments have something to be said for them, but what makes BCE (it stands for Bell Canada Enterprises) Place fascinating is the way it discloses the city's history, simultaneously revealing the old city and the new in a few sweeping glances. This is where anyone can happily start an investigation of downtown Toronto.

At the southeast corner of the complex, Yonge and Front Streets, sits the rococo 1885 Bank of Montreal, once the city's most imposing bank, possibly the inspiration for Stephen Leacock's famous essay on the terrors of opening an account. Huge towers to the north make the Bank of Montreal look like a doll house, but it's been exquisitely restored and now houses part of the Hockey Hall

This delirious Bank of Montreal went up in 1885, when banks thought giddy neoclassical architecture appropriate; today it's the Hockey Hall of Fame. And wait till you see the inside!

OPPOSITE: *The Flatiron Building, which in 1882 began its life at Wellington Street and Front as the Gooderham Building, poses elegantly against the modernist towers to the west.*

of Fame. Just a few feet north on Yonge there's a row of 19th-century storefronts, lovingly restored so that they provide a memory of old Toronto while serving the new. Inside BCE Place, the layering of history becomes more unusual. In the galleria, the steel-glass-and-granite walkway that connects BCE Place's two towers and runs from Bay Street to Yonge Street, you encounter a large surprise, a building-within-a-building, the Commercial Bank of the Midland District, originally built for nearby Wellington Street. It was taken apart, restored, and then installed in this new location, where it's an indoor sculpture and a monument to its own history. Soaring above it is the most remarkable piece of sculpture produced in Toronto in recent years, the white-painted steel hoops designed by the Spanish architect-engineer Santiago Calatrava. This archway, and the roof that Calatrava and the architects put above it, together form one of the noblest spaces in Canada.

That's the lovely part of BCE Place. The unlovely part is the exterior of the Canada Trust tower, which rises fifty-one storeys in the form of an eight-pointed star. All those angles create an astonishing number of rooms whose occupants believe they have achieved that ancient goal of corporate striving, the corner office. In fact, a visit to one of those offices will demonstrate that this architectural fiction is altogether believable. Unfortunately, it also makes the exterior look astoundingly awkward, probably the least felicitous addition to the Toronto skyline in a generation.

Among modern downtown structures, the SkyDome—completed in 1989—stands at the other end of the aesthetic scale from BCE Place. Where BCE Place soars, the SkyDome squats. Where BCE Place expresses subtlety and ingenuity, the SkyDome bluntly asserts itself. One of the few sports stadia built downtown in a big city in recent years, it's become a great generator of local enthusiasm, the home of the Blue Jays, twice World Series champions. The gigantic sculptures on the building's exterior—made by Michael Snow, the most admired artist living in Toronto—emphasize the SkyDome's in-your-face assertiveness.

Toronto's two major icons of recent decades pose together —the CN Tower, the world's tallest free-standing tourist attraction, and the Blue Jays' SkyDome.

Nearby, the CN Tower is a dizzy, extravagant monument to a dream that died. Around 1970 the Canadian National Railway planned a series of gargantuan buildings stretching across the bottom of the city, the largest construction project in Canadian history, with the CN Tower as logo. The other buildings were cancelled, but the tower went ahead anyway, and was topped off in 1976. It became a hugely profitable tourist attraction as it turned into the city's main symbol.

On King Street two kinds of 1960s modern architecture stare warily at each other, as if still in competition for the imagination of the future. To the south is the black steel-and-glass T-D Centre designed by Ludwig Mies van der Rohe (1886–1969), its main tower and its beautiful ground-level banking hall still looking as powerful and authoritative as they did when they opened in 1967. On the north side of King Street is First Canadian Place, the home of the Bank of Montreal, a very different thing entirely. The designer here is another American, Edward Durell Stone (1902–1978), who in the 1960s was offering polished, luxurious designs; the lavish use of marble gives the building a feeling of intensely focused wealth.

In the 1950s, Torontonians came to think that their old city hall, opened in 1899, needed a replacement; more important, the city needed a central public

Saved from the wreckers in the 1960s, the Old City Hall, designed by E. J. Lennox, retains its robust Romanesque power.

gathering place. Toronto set up an international competition that drew 532 entries from around the world. The winner, Viljo Revell of Finland, provided precisely what was required. The elegant concrete towers of his city hall, opened in 1965, brought a stylish, ambitious new spirit to Toronto public life. Nathan Phillips Square, also designed by Revell, gave Toronto for the first time a great piazza in the European tradition.

The Revell building helped create an atmosphere in which firms like Zeidler Roberts could operate. Eberhard Zeidler has been the main architectural force behind a dozen major projects, from Ontario Place to the Eaton Centre. In the mid-1990s Zeidler Roberts finished the astonishing Princess Margaret Hospital, a cancer treatment and research centre that feels like anything but a hospital. Hiding behind the old Ontario Hydro building on dour University Avenue, it demonstrates the patient-friendly atrium style that Zeidler favours.

Downtown Toronto began its life at what was then the edge of Lake Ontario, around Front and Church Streets. It was a harbour city, built on the shore plain next to the water, and downtown development slowly spread out to fill the plain. Today, four 19th-century structures illustrate how remnants of historic Toronto are surviving into the 21st century. At Mill Street and Trinity Street, in the eastern corner of the old downtown industrial district, the Gooderham and Worts distillery is a collection of buildings the size of a small village. It's a rarity, a well-preserved industrial complex that dates back to the middle of the 19th century and earlier. In recent decades, after its manufacturing processes (from whisky to soap) closed down, everyone continued to love it but no one knew what to do with it. In the late 1990s developers began moving it slowly toward a new life as a condominium community.

The Cathedral Church of St. James' went up at Church and King Streets in 1853, when this was the natural site for the main church of the Anglicans, the main denomination of Toronto. Frederick Cumberland, a leading Toronto architect, created a powerful English Gothic church with a 306-foot spire that remains the highest in Canada (and the second-highest in North America, after St. Patrick's in New York). But the district around the cathedral grew distinctly unfashionable by the middle of the 20th century, and St. James' (like the Metropolitan United to the north and St. Michael's, still farther north) was isolated in a rundown district. In recent decades life has come back to the streets around St. James'—symbolized by the Toronto Sculpture Garden on King Street, and the more recent Court House Square Park, just to the north and west.

Farther west, the Flatiron Building, at 49 Wellington Street East, has become a favourite among history-laden buildings in Toronto. Its place in the affections of the city is due in part to the curious triangular shape (a response to the limited site), in part to its location (at the edge of a park, where Front and Wellington Streets converge), and in part to the witty, fool-the-eye mural that Derek Michael Besant painted on its west wall in 1980—a work of art that was lovingly restored in the 1990s and is now as cherished as the old building itself.

Finally, the heart of Toronto contains one 19th-century building, Osgoode Hall, that not only looks much as it did in the Victorian age, but also plays precisely the role for which it was created. Built in stages, from the early 1830s to the late 1890s (two extensions to the back were added in the 20th century), Osgoode was intended to serve as headquarters for the Law Society of Upper Canada. It still does just that, as well as housing the Supreme Court of Ontario. It sits beautifully on the street, but the interior

A sublimely self-possessed temple from the 19th century, Osgoode Hall houses the legal profession and the Supreme Court of Ontario.

is, if anything, even more delightful. Sometimes an office worker from one of the nearby buildings, without legal business to do, will walk idly through the foyer and pause, just for a moment, to cool the soul in an atmosphere of rare serenity.

Santiago Calatrava's light-filled galleria in BCE Place. Toronto town planner Ken Greenberg says: "There's a spiritual dimension to the place that makes anyone walking there feel dignified, somehow bigger. It enhances people's lives."

Sharing space with the grandeur of the BCE Place arch is the Commercial Bank of the Midland District, designed by William Thomas in Greek Revival style on Wellington Street in the 1840s. It was disassembled and moved into BCE Place in the early 1990s.

Toronto Island has always provided the best vantage-point for anyone wanting to enjoy the skyline. In recent years the show has grown steadily more entertaining.

The CN Tower was part of a land-development project that failed to get going, but it turned out to be a success as a tourist attraction anyway. Michael Snow, asked to make sculpture for the SkyDome, produced grotesque contemporary equivalents of the gargoyles on medieval cathedrals.

The SkyDome, up close and powerful (opposite page), or far-off and glamorous on a summer night, has become one of the signature images of Toronto.

DOWNTOWN: THE LAYERED CITY ON THE SHORE PLAIN

The beauty of simplicity: High Modernist design at its most emphatic and confident, the T-D Centre by Ludwig Mies van der Rohe has established itself as a historic masterpiece of International Style architecture.

Created as the Toronto home of the Bank of Montreal, the First Bank Tower of First Canadian Place shows the lush marbled grandeur that made its architect, Edward Durell Stone, a corporate favourite in the 1960s.

In 1965, the New City Hall designed by a Finnish architect, Viljo Revell, helped change Toronto's self-image and kick-started an era of audacious architectural design.

The Flatiron Building, jammed into the triangle created by the meeting of Front and Wellington Streets, went up in 1892, a decade before the similar building in New York. The much-admired 1980 mural is the work of a Calgary artist, Derek Michael Besant.

The Gooderham and Worts distillery is an assembly of ancient industrial buildings, abandoned by the industry that used them. A famous site, it is rarely visited but often seen—pressed into service for television shows and movies, it has served as everything from an Old West town to a Second World War Polish village. It's scheduled to become a collection of condominium buildings.

Unlikely as it seems, this light, airy atrium is in a cancer centre, the high-rise Princess Margaret Hospital, which was inserted into a narrow space on University Avenue in the 1990s. This is the higher atrium, for research; the space at lower right that looks like a swimming pool is actually a skylight for the bottom atrium, which serves outpatients.

The Cathedral Church of St. James', a serious building for a serious age (gravitas in every brick); Toronto's Anglican mother church was designed in the late 1840s by the architect Frederick Cumberland, to the requirements of Bishop John Strachan, the spiritual leader of early Victorian Toronto.

Inside Osgoode Hall (above and opposite page), the centre of Ontario justice, the atmosphere is restrained and elegant, sheltered from the tension of the streets outside.

ON THE GRAND OLD STEETS OF TORONTO

Sheriff William Botsford Jarvis went into Toronto history for two reasons. The first was his leadership of a platoon of riflemen on the government side in the uprising of December 1837—stationing his troops at the farm of a Mrs. Sharpe Sharpe (about where College Street now meets Yonge), he turned back the rebels led by William Lyon Mackenzie. He also founded Rosedale, and named it. In 1824 William and Mary Jarvis acquired a house to the north of the city, with 150 acres attached. Mary, so the story goes, called it "Rosedale" because of the wild roses they found blooming there. In the 1850s Jarvis laid out Park Road and built a bridge across the ravine, to connect his property to the new Village of Yorkville. He then subdivided 100 acres into sixty-two building lots on seven curving streets.

This was the moment when Rosedale acquired its peculiar geography, which Torontonians from more ordered districts find baffling. Where the rest of the city was laid out in a military-style grid plan, Rosedale's streets followed the natural topography. This was either because Jarvis respected nature or because it would have cost far too much to do otherwise.

In its early days, Rosedale property development was not the success its promoters hoped it would be. Torontonians of today often call Rosedale houses "Victorian," but in fact few of them were built before the death of the old queen in 1901. The Toronto economy was sluggish in the late 19th century, and in any case Rosedale was inconvenient: it was too distant for most people. But in the Edwardian period, when roads and the economy both improved, Rosedale property became highly desirable. In the first years of the century, it was a boom neighbourhood, pulling the rich and the upper-middle class away from downtown Sherbourne Street and Jarvis Street. By 1914, when the beginning of the Great War brought construction to a stop, most of

What better symbol for a Rosedale house than a stone lion?

OPPOSITE: Many Toronto districts feel like intimate villages, but the Annex makes the ideal of neighbourhood into a religion.

Rosedale as we know it was built. Since then it has evolved as a place of wondrous legend, the true home of Old Money, a district with its own accent (a characteristic honk, so it's said), where characters who have stepped out of Robertson Davies novels can be seen walking their dogs through the labyrinthine streets.

Rosedale people are proud of their district, but quiet about it. Over in the Annex, people feel so strongly about the neighbourhood that it often seems they speak of little else. There's a reason. In the early 1970s it was the focus of the successful city-wide struggle against a Metropolitan Toronto plan to drive the Spadina Expressway through to downtown. Many districts would have been hurt, but the Annex would have suffered most and therefore remembers that historic event with a burning intensity. How strongly do Annex people feel about neighbourhood preservation? Consider this: in 1996 they did everything but take up arms when they were threatened with the loss of a single café. A landlord cancelled the lease of Dooney's, a Bloor Street restaurant favoured by littérateurs and other hyper-articulate Annex dwellers, so that he could rent to Starbucks at a higher rate. The Annex treated this as a major affront to Western civilization. Four newspaper columnists (two in *The Toronto Star*, two in *The Globe and Mail*) wrote impassioned commentary, one *Star* writer implying ominously that Starbucks would find itself in trouble with the city health bureaucracy if it insisted on bringing its insane plan for world conquest to this sacred corner of Bloor Street. Another columnist kept returning obsessively to Dooney's, as if it were the Canadian constitution. Starbucks, mortified by this negative attention, backed off, and Dooney's was saved.

This happened in the very heart of Jane Jacobs country, where the word *neighbourhood* is pronounced with reverence. Jacobs, an ex-American who became a world-famous writer on urbanism with her 1961 book, *Death and*

Annex residents rose in righteous fury when Dooney's, a café beloved by the intelligentsia, was briefly threatened by Starbucks.

Life of Great American Cities, settled on Albany Avenue, one of the key residential streets of the Annex, in 1970. In the decades that followed, she became the patron saint of local urban thinking, in particular the kind of thinking that emphasizes the texture of neighbourhoods.

For those who love architecture, the streets of the Annex provide one of the great free shows in Toronto.

History has given the Annex not only a passionate sense of self-protection, but also a rather exotic reputation, based in part on close links to the academic world, York University and Ryerson as well as the nearby University of Toronto. So many Annex couples consist of two academics that on some streets there are said to be more professors than houses. From the beginning the Annex has been favoured by professors—in fact, it was built in the 1880s to attract the growing class of professionals. A developer named Simeon Janes laid out the area bounded by Bathurst, Avenue Road, Bloor, and Dupont, and organized the lots on the most notable streets, including Bedford, Admiral, Madison, and Huron.

The district rose to eminence before the turn of the century, acquiring its rather ordinary name from the fact that it was annexed by the city in 1887. It fell precipitously after the First World War, eclipsed by Rosedale, Forest Hill, and several other places. Many of the finest houses were destroyed for apartment buildings in the postwar boom, but there are still scores of them, and many architecture-loving Torontonians can pass a happy afternoon walking the Annex streets and identifying the Victorian, Edwardian, Georgian, Queen Anne, and other designs permanently on display. Margaret Atwood, a famous Annex resident for many years, caught the architectural spirit of the district in *The Robber Bride*, when the professor heroine goes out in the morning and "turns to look back at her house, as she often does, admiring it. . . . brick, late Victorian, tall and narrow, with green fish-scale shingles on its upper third. Her study window looks out from the fake tower on the left: the Victorians loved to think they were living in castles. . . . A solid house, reassuring; a fort, a bastion, a keep."

Among all the grand old surviving houses of the Annex, one especially demands to be noticed: 135 St. George Street, an elegantly turreted and gabled redbrick mansion in the Richardsonian Romanesque style. David Roberts designed it in 1892 for the most powerful Torontonian of the age, George Gooderham, a whisky baron and the head of the Bank of Toronto. After his death it was sold to the York Club, which has since 1909 maintained it with the care deserved by what many consider the most beautiful house ever built in Toronto.

Parkdale has a history as old as the Annex's, but less happy in recent times. If you go along Queen Street and proceed west of Dufferin, you enter what was, in the 1880s, the village of Parkdale, which was founded as a suburb that took advantage of the cool summer breezes off Lake Ontario. In its great days, which lasted past the First World War, people spoke of Parkdale in the same way they spoke of Rosedale, as a place of good houses on handsome, tree-lined streets. But a series of calamities fell upon Parkdale: it never recovered from the Depression, and it was crippled in the 1950s when the Gardiner Expressway chewed up some of the finest houses and cut Parkdale off from the lake. But many good houses remain (the residents like to say you get more house there for the money than anywhere else in Toronto).

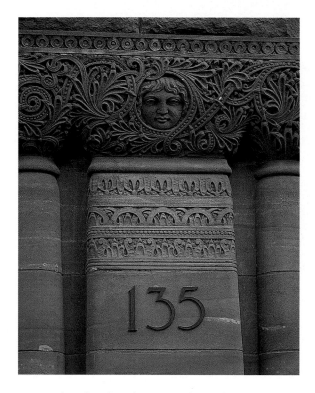

Every detail is handsome at the York Club on St. George Street.

Parkdale contains Toronto's most remarkable little exercise in urban nostalgia, a cluster of seven row houses called Melbourne Place. Built in the 1880s, the houses were renovated by a history-loving developer in the 1960s. The people who bought them turned their street into a highly self-conscious piece of the 19th century. They put in a road surface of brick, installed decorative iron gates at the entrance to the street, put up huge hanging baskets of flowers, and added a communal picnic table. As the finishing touch, they bought two gas streetlights (antiques from Scotland) and hooked them up to the gas system so that they perpetually flicker. The result makes people think of Charles Dickens or Sherlock Holmes. For the residents, the $15 a month these extras cost is a small price to pay for the looks of astonishment on the faces of visitors when they see it for the first time. For connoisseurs of the old residential Toronto, Melbourne Place is a wonderful curiosity: a tiny corner of the gaslight era survives, providing precisely the sort of surprise that awaits those who set out to explore the city.

Behind the gates of Parkdale's Melbourne Place, startled visitors plunge into the 19th century.

In Rosedale, even a little covered bridge manages to achieve a poetic style.

At dusk, when the antique globes light up, Rosedale streets take on a charm all their own.

Long the true home of *Old Money*, Rosedale is the only Toronto district to maintain its status from the first years of the 20th century to the last.

Possibly the finest private house ever built in Toronto, turreted 135 St. George Street—designed in 1892 by David Roberts as George Gooderham's home—became the York Club in 1909.

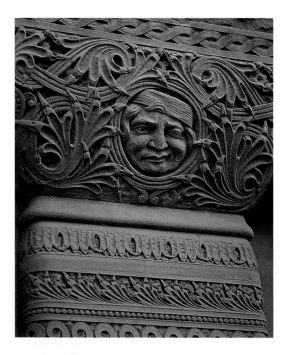

On a solid and solemn building, a sculptured sense of comedy.

In the Annex, the streets are designed to create a sense of civility and neighbourly goodwill.

The home–owners on Melbourne Place in Parkdale imported antique gas streetlights from Scotland.

Although literally "gated," Melbourne Place in fact welcomes visitors from outside.

PLACES OF PRIDE AND CELEBRATION

EW TORONTONIANS, particularly those who came to the city from far-off places like Hong Kong or New Delhi, seldom express surprise at the public manifestations of group identity that are now commonplace in Toronto. Back home, it's normal for masses of people to walk on the streets as a way of making a point or articulating pleasure. But to old Torontonians, reared by a different ethic, the highly public Toronto that took shape from the 1970s to the 1990s remains strange—jarring, startling, and in many ways a source of wonderment and pleasure.

Only a generation ago, Toronto was an essentially private city, not much given to displays of pride in anything. There were exceptions, but they were not the specific expressions of any group. The Canadian National Exhibition, which originated as an agricultural fair in the 1840s and eventually became (Torontonians used to say with pride) "the world's largest annual outdoor exhibition," has been an end-of-summer highlight for generations. The Royal Agricultural Winter Fair, often graced by royalty, has always been a great moment for the horsy set. But in these events cultural differences were muted, if not disdained; few imagined that it was anyone's duty to state them publicly. The most blatant assertions of identity were the annual parade of the Orange Lodges commemorating the Battle of the Boyne on July 12, the parade organized by the unions on Labour Day—and, in a quite different way, the Santa Claus Parade in late autumn that traditionally signalled the onset of winter and the start of serious Christmas shopping.

But today Toronto is a place where pride and public self-assertion are part of everyday life. The annual Caribana parade, to take the most spectacular

At Caribana, only the gorgeous is acceptable.

OPPOSITE: The Princes' Gates at the Canadian National Exhibition, dedicated to King George V's two sons, defined neoclassical architecture as Toronto (and the then-famous firm of Chapman and Oxley) saw it in 1927.

example, is by a long way the most ambitious public expression of black culture in North America. Started as a way of unifying West Indian immigrants in Toronto, it has spread out to encompass black culture of many different origins. Making the magnificent floats and costumes for the parade has turned into a local art form and industry.

Gay Pride Day has become an event on a similarly grand scale. One Sunday every spring, a long strip of Church Street, the centre of the gay ghetto, closes to traffic. Booths, food sellers, and rock bands fill the road, and every conceivable variety of gay life, from cross-dressers to Gay Presbyterians, comes forth to express itself. The climax of the day is a parade that usually includes major local politicians, whose presence is testimony that gays have created their own effective community.

In the late 1990s the Jewish community organized its own parade, as part of the annual Ashkenaz Festival. It begins close to what was once the heart of Jewish Toronto, Kensington Market, and proceeds to Harbourfront for concerts, art exhibitions, and Jewish cuisine. Harbourfront has played a key role in changing Toronto from a private to a public city. It was called into being by the federal government in the 1970s, having been announced by Prime Minister Pierre Trudeau as one of the "goodies" (his word) offered during an election campaign. The government brought together a collection of underused or abandoned buildings and lots, and put marinas, theatres, and galleries on them. Miraculously,

Greek culture has helped transform Toronto—and the Danforth.

it worked. Part ongoing festival, part arts centre, part flea market, Harbourfront became a vital meeting place for the city.

There are other year-round festivals, though they aren't given that name. Danforth Avenue—always called "the Danforth" by Torontonians —is a year-round festival of Greek cuisine, its open-air cafés particularly lively in summer. St. Clair Avenue West, which also has a collection of sidewalk cafés, seems on some nights to be a little strip of Milan inserted into Toronto.

And Spadina Avenue has been a place of identity-assertion for as long as anyone can remember; the identities keep changing, but not the assertion. Early in this century it was the grand boulevard of Jewish culture as well as the trading centre of the garment industry. In the 1950s it became an immigration-receiving area for Hungarian and other East European immigrants. In 1970 there was only one Chinese restaurant the length and breadth of the avenue, but in the next fifteen years Spadina and its ancillary streets turned into the largest of Toronto's four Chinatowns. More recently, it has accommodated large numbers of Vietnamese as well. In the summer of 1997, when the new street-car line was put into service, the city celebrated by erecting a series of sculptures recalling various moments in Spadina's history. This was explained as a way to give the street character. But as it happened, Spadina of all the streets in the Toronto area was the one that least needed that sort of help.

High above Spadina Avenue and its streetcar line, emblematic sculptures illustrate the street's remarkable history.

For generations the Canadian National Exhibition was the climax of the Toronto summer, but in the last few decades of the 20th century it was overshadowed by more exuberant events. It remains, however, the biggest thing of its kind in the whole damn world, as any Old Torontonian will point out.

PLACES OF PRIDE AND CELEBRATION

At the Royal Agricultural Winter Fair every year, the elite of Toronto emerges from its castles in Rosedale, Forest Hill, and Don Mills to celebrate its own existence.

The Santa Claus Parade, for generations the most famous publicity stunt of the Eaton's department-store chain, has in recent years been taken over by a group of local companies. It remains a milestone in the Toronto year.

PLACES OF PRIDE AND CELEBRATION

There is nothing anywhere else to equal Caribana, a celebration of black art and pride that every year draws tens of thousands of visitors to Toronto for one exciting weekend.

PLACES OF PRIDE AND CELEBRATION

In the 1950s Danforth Avenue, east of the Don Valley, was what it had been for generations: a run-down, predictable commercial street serving the old houses of Riverdale. Then, at some point in the 1960s, the first Greek immigrants settled there, and soon were joined by many more. They opened restaurants that the rest of Toronto quickly came to adore. Though many of the original Greeks have moved on to the suburbs, the effervescent strip they created lives on.

No one knows whose idea it was, but in the 1970s the federal government decided to make the waterfront land it owned into a vast community centre. The result is Harbourfront, an agreeably chaotic agglomeration of galleries, concert stages, theatres, marinas, and restaurants. It's so casual that a visitor would never guess that Ottawa created the whole thing.

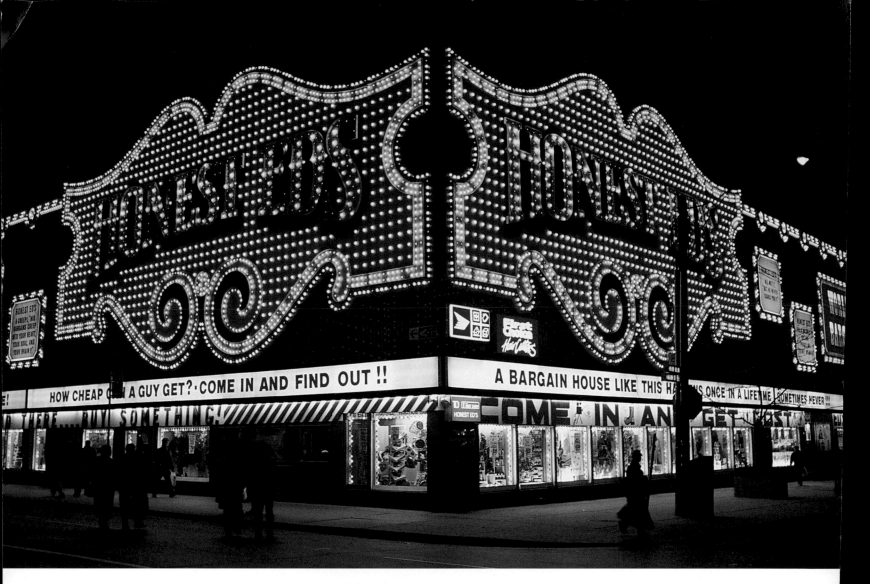

This magnificent Pop Art object is Honest Ed's, the discount store where the Ed Mirvish empire began.

And this is the section of Markham Street next to Honest Ed's, now Mirvish Village.

And here, downtown on King Street, is one of Ed's provinces: two first-class theatres and a clutch of restaurants.

PLACES OF PRIDE AND CELEBRATION

When the great Yiddish writer Isaac Bashevis Singer visited Toronto in the late 1930s, he thought Spadina Avenue was a piece of Jewish Warsaw miraculously transported to the new world. It was then already a running festival of ethnic assertion, with its Yiddish theatre and Yiddish newspapers. Today it's the core of Toronto's largest Chinatown, a street that is deeply conscious of its history as a place of new beginnings.

Until suddenly it happened, no one predicted that Mississauga, too, could have a Chinatown, just like Toronto and Scarborough.

A wall in Mississauga echoes the style of a whole culture.

And what's a Chinatown, after all, without a pagoda?

Places of Pride and Celebration

WORLDS OF ART AND LEARNING

ORLEY CALLAGHAN, who was for decades the most celebrated novelist in Toronto, wrote in 1948 that the front campus of the University of Toronto, his old school, "seems to be a village green.…It looks like an old town. And is too. It is a university town there in the heart of a big industrial city." Years ago, people stopped speaking of Toronto as an industrial city, but the main burden of Callaghan's statement remains true—truer, in fact, than in 1948. The university stands at the heart of Toronto, geographically, spiritually, and professionally. When it was founded in the 19th century it was north of the city, but Toronto has long since surrounded it. Now it's embedded in the city, a layer of learning and ambition that touches every corner of Toronto life in one way or another. It is also a place of considerable pride. The University of Toronto, it has been said, is one of the 100 universities on the planet which believe they are in the top 20.

As the biggest property owner in the city, the university possesses some of the best and worst architecture. On the front campus, older usually means better. In fact, the best building is also the most venerable, Frederick Cumberland's Romanesque masterpiece, University College, finished in 1859. It embodies all the Romanesque virtues, from a graceful shape to superb stone carving and the most magnificent doorway in Toronto. When the university decided on Gothic

Revival, it built the best, Henry Sproatt's Hart House (1919). There are wonderfully planned sections of the university, too, like the Protestant-to-Catholic walk east of Queen's Park, where the visitor can amble through a series of Victoria College (United Church) buildings and then through the precincts of St. Michael's College, the Basilian fathers' Roman Catholic school. Here and in the

There are those who say University College is Toronto's handsomest building, and the doorway its greatest asset.

OPPOSITE: *At the Art Gallery of Ontario, the Tanenbaum Sculpture Atrium turned out to be among the noblest spaces created in Toronto.*

various chapels, including the lovely Trinity College chapel on Hoskin Avenue, we are reminded that for many years the university was essentially a federation of religious colleges.

Modern times have not been so good to university architecture—Sidney Smith Hall, a depressing modernist building from the 1960s, is sadly typical. But the refurbishment of St. George Street, accompanied by several fine new buildings, has raised hopes that the university could once again be reshaped as a beautiful urban environment. In any case, there are a few gems from the last few decades, the most notable being Massey College, the 1960s masterpiece of Ron Thom, with a quadrangle that reworks ancient European forms for modern Canada.

In 1996 the university opened a hidden treasure, a remarkable collection of art ranging from a Matisse drawing to a lovely Adam and Eve by Lucas Cranach the Elder to Russian icons. It was assembled over a lifetime by Dr. Lillian

Ever since this sandstone-faced east wing went up in 1931–32, the Royal Ontario Museum has been a central force in Toronto culture.

Malcove, a Ukraine-born, Winnipeg-raised psychiatrist who in 1933 became the first woman accredited as a Freudian analyst in New York. She never lived in Toronto and had no connections with the university, but she wanted the collection kept together and chose to leave it to Toronto. Today it's handsomely installed in the new University Art Centre on the University College quadrangle.

At the northeast corner of the university sits the Royal Ontario Museum, a public gallery and scholarly research centre that is intimately linked to the university by the fact that all the curators are also professors. For many Torontonians over the last seventy-five years, the ROM has been the real centre of the city, the local treasure-house, the home of ancient Chinese tombs, the great British Columbia totem pole that dominates the main staircase, and many thousands of other objects.

The ROM's rival for the attention of the city, the Art Gallery of Ontario (AGO), has for generations been the main showplace in Toronto for painting and sculpture. Today it contains—along with the Henry Moore Centre and the Grange, that remarkable early-19th-century mansion—one of the most exhilarating spaces created in the 1990s, the Tanenbaum Sculpture Atrium, in which the history of the building (including the Grange and the Renaissance-style 1920s art gallery) can be seen in one glimpse.

Behind the Art Gallery of Ontario, the Grange presents a façade of Georgian gentility.

Of all the hundreds of spaces for art in the Toronto area, surely the most outlandish is the sculpture park at the Guild Inn in Scarborough, where the owners have installed a bizarre collection of art objects in all shapes and sizes, many of them collected from Toronto buildings destroyed in the 1950s and 1960s. This is the elephant burial ground of local taste. Some of the cultural debris, mainly Greek pillars, has been assembled into an outdoor theatre. The rest is placed around the grounds, where visitors wander in a post-modern daze, perhaps pondering the meaning of all this high-toned clutter. It's a haphazard collection, carrying no explicit message, but it would be hard to visit it without experiencing rueful thoughts about the future of all the brilliant and original buildings Toronto has erected in our own time.

Where sculpture goes to die: Scarborough's Guild Inn.

In the 1850s, Frederick Cumberland, one of the great stars of Toronto architecture, produced his masterpiece, University College, still the historic heart of the University of Toronto.

One of the few great Toronto buildings of the 1960s, Massey College was designed by Ron Thom, with the advice of the college's founding master, Robertson Davies.

Named for Hart Massey, founder of the farm-implements family, Hart House at the University of Toronto embodies the best in Late Gothic Revival.

OPPOSITE: *In the 1950s, the University of Toronto's Trinity College imported Sir Giles Gilbert Scott from England to create its chapel; the result became one of the most admired buildings on campus, right down to the stone details.*

In the octagonal rotunda beyond the front door of the Royal Ontario Museum, a golden mosaic ceiling inspired by the museum's first director, C.T. Currelly, hints at the cultural riches to be found inside.

One of four majestic totem poles in the ROM stairwells, this 24.5-metre-high
Nisga'a sculpture was first raised at Nass River, B.C., around 1870. Abandoned in
the 1920s after its makers moved elsewhere, it was cut into three pieces for shipping
to Toronto. In 1933 the ROM was built around it.

A **Walking Woman** *sculpture by Michael Snow (lower right) finds a place in the George Weston Hall, entrance to the Art Gallery of Ontario's most recent (1992) renovation.*

After it opened in the early 1990s, the Tanenbaum Atrium—which links the old version of the Art Gallery of Ontario with the Grange—quickly became the gallery's most popular space.

Henry Moore himself designed the entire Moore Centre in the 1970s, from the room's shape to the placing of the sculptures and even the colour of the walls.

WORLDS OF ART AND LEARNING

Easily the country's most eccentric sculpture park, the Guild Inn assembles the detritus of Toronto's yesterdays.

The architect Ron Thom and the critic Herbert Whittaker assembled chunks of demolished neoclassical buildings into a Greek theatre for the Guild.

Mingling discarded past with creative present, the Guild assembles random bits of architectural history alongside sculpture by current artists.

THE CITY'S UNFOLDING SEASONS

RING-BILLED GULLS, so populous in Toronto that one day they will surely be placed on the city's coat of arms, know just what to do when winter approaches: they head south. Tens of thousands of ring-billed gulls have been born in Toronto every summer since their ancestors discovered, in the 1970s, that their dream home was the Leslie Street Spit, a bit of human-created wilderness that juts into the lake from east-downtown Toronto. Even so, it's not their idea of a year-round residence. As the air turns cold, the gulls head for the east coast of Florida, and so also do many Toronto humans.

But for the majority of Torontonians, neither gulls nor affluent citizens nor pensioners, winter is the deadliest time. It has its moments, of course. At 6 a.m. after a heavy night-time snow, the streets of Rosedale or Scarborough or Parkdale acquire a breathtaking beauty. The stillness is worth savouring. But within an hour or two, automobiles have turned the snow into brown slush, the sidewalks are dangerously slippery, and the city is facing, once again, the truth: winter is not a season but a syndrome, an ever-recurring urban depression, a many-months-long-oh-God-will-it-never-end Municipal Problem.

But if winter is Toronto's problem, the Metro Zoo is Toronto's favourite on-site solution. This vast zoological garden in Scarborough, inevitably labelled "world class" by local enthusiasts when it was created in the 1970s, has become the place where Torontonians go when they decide that if they can't beat winter, they'll join it. Aside from space for caging animals, and many spaces for letting them range over what appears to be wilderness, there's a vast open region for recreation. When the snow is on the ground you can see the most vigorous of the citizenry cross-country skiing

On the other hand, it's hard to make the case for winter in downtown Toronto.

OPPOSITE: *Autumn in the ravines of Toronto makes even an expressway—in this case the Don Valley Parkway—into a work of art designed by nature.*

Edwards Gardens, situated in one of Toronto's many ravines, is well worth a visit in the spring.

on the Zoo grounds, combining winter exercise with a visit to the exotic animals. Aside from Metro Zoo, the best place in Toronto to appreciate snow is Mount Pleasant Cemetery, which was founded in 1876 and fills an enormous piece of land in what is now the centre of the city, northeast of St. Clair Avenue and Yonge Street. The tombstones and monuments of significant Torontonians —including Glenn Gould, Sir Frederick Banting, Mackenzie King, and various Eatons —look especially handsome when encrusted with snow. (And at any time of year, Mount Pleasant, where the air is thick with history, repays a visit.)

Spring in Toronto will always be a disappointment to those brought up on English poetry: no one will ever say, "Oh, to be in Rosedale, now that April's here"—since April in Rosedale, or anywhere else in Toronto, conforms to no one's idea of spring. For that matter, the early days of May are often unspringlike, and when spring finally arrives it turns out to be fleeting. Almost immediately after the first southern birds appear and the first sniff of spring comes from the trees, the air grows hot. Summer begins.

And that is worth waiting for, the first of our two good seasons. It can be appreciated anywhere in Toronto, but in three places especially. The Beach district, the southeastern end of old Toronto, looks as if it were precisely designed for summer, which is in fact the case. It started life shortly after 1900 as cottage country for downtown residents, and many high-priced Beach houses are converted cottages. The mile of sandy beach on Lake Ontario and the network of parks make it feel like a resort community still, and in summer the long boardwalk becomes social centre and main street. The giddy Queen Street strip of stores, restaurants, and bars has the distinct air of a beach town in Florida or southern California, an elaborate act of defiance in the face of the Canadian climate.

Although the harbour has never become the busy port Toronto once planned, summer turns it into one of the great pleasure centres.

The Toronto islands, that wonderful archipelago on the southern side of the harbour, also began life as a summer resort and today exist mainly as parkland. To go there on the ferry from the hot city is to experience a kind of miracle, a twenty-minute ride from tension to tranquillity. On Ward's Island, at the archipelago's eastern end, visitors discover hundreds of year-round residents whose private houses and gardens bring a sense of human spontaneity to what might otherwise be a sterile public park.

Gardens are crucial, too, in Cabbagetown. That's where the Toronto summer makes its most poetic statement, at once densely urban and village-like. In summer the residential streets of Cabbagetown close in around the visitor: blooms are everywhere, trees are in full leaf, bushes are flowering, and the streets seem narrow. Walk along the eastern reaches of Carlton Street, or walk up Sackville Street, and you feel yourself drawn into an intimate relationship with all that carefully nurtured flora. The scents of

Once derelict, the Cabbagetown district sprang to new life in the 1970s.

THE CITY'S UNFOLDING SEASONS

roses and clematis, lavender and lobelia, hang in the air, and in the evenings you can smell the lilies. This district was down-at-the-heels and nearly dead as recently as 1970. Today it's one of the liveliest places in Toronto—especially when summer brings every street vividly to life.

But the best of all Toronto seasons is autumn, which starts just after the Canadian National Exhibition closes down at Labour Day and lasts until the first snow flies. Autumn is when Torontonians rediscover their greatest natural asset, the hundreds of ravines that were cut into the land by streams and rivers flowing

toward Lake Ontario at the end of the last Ice Age. Toronto, it's sometimes said, is not a city with parks but a park that contains a city. Visitors don't easily see this, since generations of city planners have ignored the ravines by building bridges over them, or running highways through them (notably the Don Valley Parkway), or filling them in for development. But nothing kills them, and now they are protected by law, and if you discover them (even just two or three of them) you could become addicted for life. They are the most unusual feature of Toronto: no other big city has so much nature woven through it. Anne Michaels, in her novel *Fugitive Pieces*, says Toronto is "a city of ravines. Remnants of wilderness have been left behind. Through these great sunken gardens you can traverse the city beneath the streets, look up to the floating neighbourhoods, houses built in the treetops."

And by early October each of the ravines turns into an open-air art gallery as the leaves on thousands of trees die the most poetic death in nature. The sap stops flowing, growth comes to an end, and as the chlorophyll disintegrates it allows carotenoids to appear in the form of powerful orange, and the alkalinity from the soil to show up as glorious red in the soft maple. This is when we recall that the Group of Seven, glorifiers of the Canadian wilderness, were mostly Toronto boys who did much of their work in their studios on the edge of the Rosedale ravine.

OPPOSITE: In autumn, brilliant colours in Rosedale ravine illustrate the uniqueness of the ravine system: no other big city has so much nature so intimately blended with its streets.

Among solutions to the miseries of winter, the Metro Zoo in Scarborough holds a high place, offering both the companionship of the animals and the exuberance of cross-country skiing.

Since it opened in the 1960s, the reflecting pool in Nathan Phillips Square (opposite) has been Toronto's favourite outdoor rink. Tobogganing in the park, on the other hand, has been part of Toronto since the beginning.

The Beach district, which began its life as a summer resort early in the 20th century, comes into its own when summer turns the boardwalk on Lake Ontario into the place to be seen.

THE CITY'S UNFOLDING SEASONS

Possibly the humblest architectural monument in all Canada, the Leuty Avenue lifeguard station was saved from destruction by militant Beach residents.

Dull and dowdy in earlier generations, the mile of Queen Street that runs through the Beach district now becomes a summertime tourist attraction.

Those who live on the Toronto islands, and those who often visit them, know that paradise is only a brief ferryboat ride from downtown.

Opposite: *On a summer day, the lagoons wander lazily through the Toronto islands archipelago.*

Only a few hundred people live there, but to the big-city visitor Ward's Island offers the charm of a community in miniature.

THE CITY'S UNFOLDING SEASONS

On Ward's Island, small houses and short streets create a unique sense of community, expressed (above) by church services the locals attend in their sailing whites.

THE CITY'S UNFOLDING SEASONS

In Cabbagetown, fiercely ambitious gardeners fill the summer air with a lingering sweetness.

THE CITY'S UNFOLDING SEASONS

In High Park, in hundreds of ravines, and in a Japanese garden, autumn stages nature's most florid death scene and asserts every year its status as monarch of the Toronto seasons.

THE CITY'S UNFOLDING SEASONS

INDEX

p